Grow
a Tomato!

by Kristin Cashore
illustrated by Nicole Wong

PEARSON
Scott
Foresman

Editorial Offices: Glenview, Illinois • Parsippany, New Jersey • New York, New York
Sales Offices: Needham, Massachusetts • Duluth, Georgia • Glenview, Illinois
Coppell, Texas • Ontario, California • Mesa, Arizona

Every effort has been made to secure permission and provide appropriate credit for photographic material. The publisher deeply regrets any omission and pledges to correct errors called to its attention in subsequent editions.

Unless otherwise acknowledged, all photographs are the property of Scott Foresman, a division of Pearson Education.

Photo locators denoted as follows: Top (T), Center (C), Bottom (B), Left (L), Right (R), Background (Bkgd)

Illustrations by Nicole Wong

ISBN: 0-328-13280-2

5 6 7 8 9 10 V010 14 13 12 11 10 09 08 07

It is always good to eat vegetables. It is also good to grow your vegetables!

Tomatoes are good vegetables for growing at home. How do you grow tomatoes?

First, plant tomato seeds in small pots. Put the pots in a warm, sunny place in your house. Water them. Soon green stems will peek out. Leaves will grow! Keep them inside for six weeks.

Outside, dig holes in the soil. Take any rocks out of the soil so that it will not be bumpy.

Slide the plants out of the pots. Be careful not to break the roots. Place them into the holes. Pat down the soil around the plants.

Tomatoes are thirsty plants. They will need water. Do not water one plant more than others. Also, do not let the soil stay dry for too long.

Fertilizer is special food for plants that helps them grow. You can buy fertilizer or make your own. Some people use food scraps and plants to make their own fertilizer called *compost*.

Tomato plants can grow quite tall. The tomato vines must be held up. If not, the tomato plants will flop on the ground. They will not get enough sun.

Wooden stakes can keep your tomato plants standing tall. As the plants grow, tie the vines to the stakes. Tie them very gently so the vines do not break.

You must also prune your tomato plants. When you prune, you trim the leaves and stems that are yellow or brown. Try to keep the plants healthy and green!

If you water, fertilize, stake, and prune your tomato plants, they will grow. White or yellow flowers will bloom. Soon, small green fruit will start to show. Tomatoes are on the way!

It is time for harvest when your tomatoes are a deep red color. Pick them. Wash them so that they are clean and smooth. Then enjoy your tomatoes!